The Travel Journal of Eliza House Trist 1783-84

KAREN A. CHASE

224 PAGES
RICHMOND, VIRGINIA

224Pages
P.O. Box 23259
Richmond, VA 23223
224Pages.com

Copyright © 2024 Karen A. Chase

All rights reserved. No part of this book may be reproduced in any form without permission in writing from the author and publisher, except by a reviewer, who may quote brief passages in reviews.

Cover & Interior Design: 224Pages

A new transcription, edited, and with an introduction
by Karen A. Chase
of
The Travel Journal Kept by Mrs. Trist
on her Journey from Philadelphia to Louisiana 1783

University of Virginia, Charlottesville
Albert & Shirley Small Special Collections
Papers of the Trist, Randolph, and Burke Families 1721-1969

THE TRAVEL JOURNAL OF
ELIZA HOUSE TRIST, 1783-84
ISBN 978-1-7337528-6-2

For

Elizabeth House Trist

*Within our founding history
— and by your own hand —
you have earned this room of your own.*

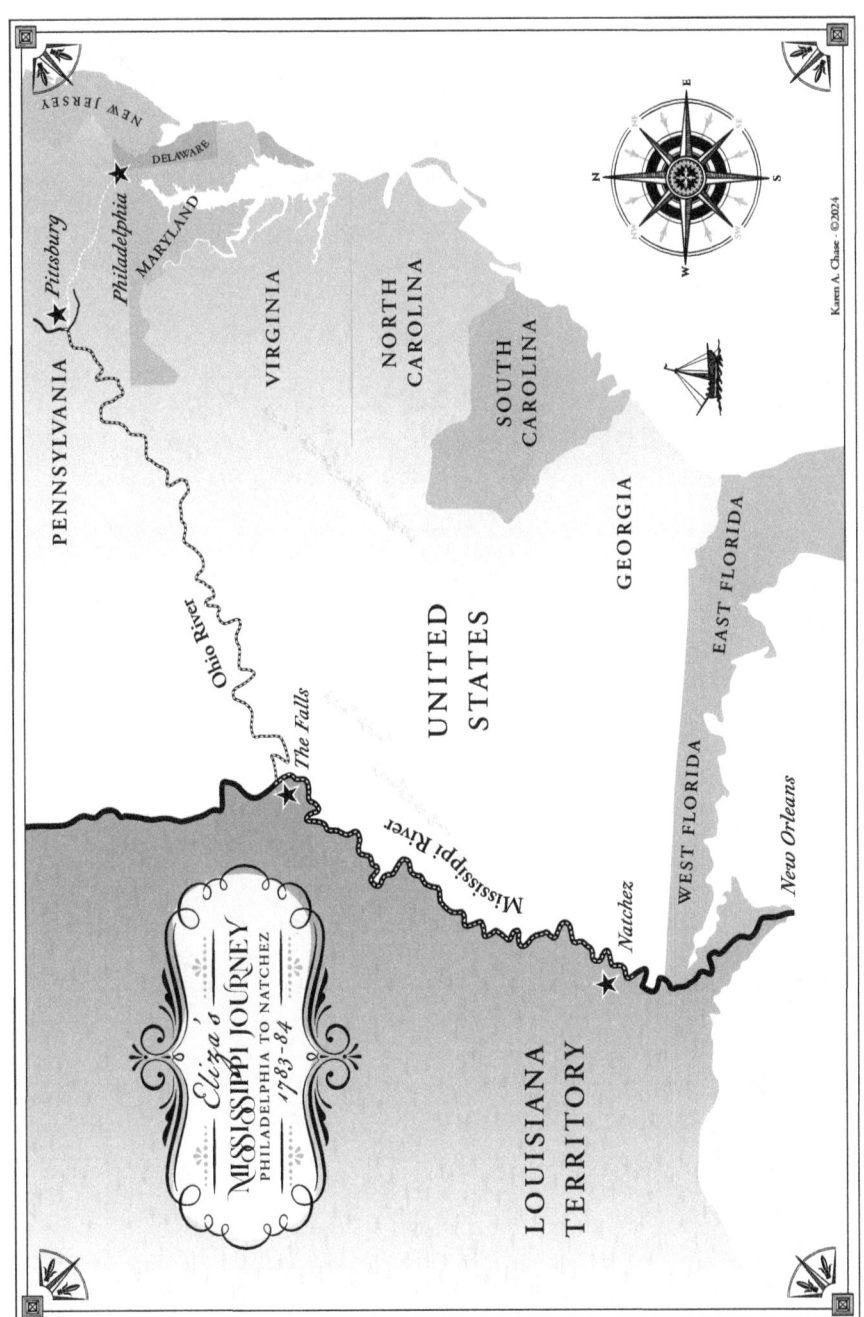

Elizabeth House Trist, 1751-1828

Silhouette Portrait by William Bache, 1741-1845
National Portrait Gallery, Smithsonian Institution;
partial gift of Sarah Bache Bloise.

To date, this is the only known portrait of Elizabeth House Trist.
In this silhouette, created in 1804, Eliza would have been about 53.
When she wrote the travel journal, she was in her early thirties.

The silhouette featured on the cover is a faithful attempt
at age regression using her original portrait, descendant portraits,
and other Bache and period sihouettes for reference.

Introduction

*Unless something unforeseen happens
I shall very soon proceed on my journey.*

*It is a very great undertaking
for me who never experiencd any hardships
to ride over the Mountains this season of the year.*

E. Trist

In a letter to Thomas Jefferson,
December, 1783

A Westward Woman

  A woman named Elizabeth House Trist traveled west in 1783, two decades before Lewis and Clark, and kept a journal for Thomas Jefferson.

  I imagine you're now asking the same questions I did upon first learning this historical fact. Who was this woman and had she been an explorer before? How did she know Thomas Jefferson? Why did she venture west in the first place?

  First, it's fair to say Elizabeth House Trist was unaccustomed to travel. Born to Samuel and Mary House in 1751,[1] Eliza Trist's roots were firmly planted in the city of her birth, Philadelphia—a city covering but a few square miles and with a population of about 30,000.

  By today's standards, that's a small town, but in Colonial times, Philadelphia was the second-largest city in America, affording many comforts.

  Eliza—as she is sometimes referenced, even by the National Archives—grew up within this burgeoning political, cultural, and intellectual hub. Her home was mere steps from the bustling port that spilled forth a plethora of oysters, trout, and perch for sale by the fishmongers on Dock Street. Ships sweeping in from the Caribbean and Europe brought spices, fabrics, and imported goods like china. Even pineapples were easily available amid the stalls lining Market Street near her home.

Eliza's father ran a dry goods business until his untimely death in 1766.[2] Her mother, Mary House—no shrinking widow—used the assets of the willed estate, appraised at more than £2200 at the time,[3] to open and run a boarding house that became widely recognized for its "fine entertainments."

The House Inn was well-regarded for its superior foods, quality linens and rooms, and an atmosphere that encouraged lively conversations. These amenities and comfortable accommodations, especially for those who might visit the city for weeks or months at a time, were attractive to many founders familiar to us now. James Madison. Silas Deane. Edward Rutledge. And, in the early pre-Revolutionary years, when coming in for Philosophical Society meetings, it was also frequented by the well-known Virginian, Thomas Jefferson.[4]

As Eliza grew older, the inn being her home, she worked alongside her mother. Many a trip was likely made to her older brother Samuel's dry goods shop on Second Street,[5] where orders were placed for candles, tea, and other much-needed supplies for the House Inn. Although no picture as yet, save the silhouette featured within these pages, is known to exist of Eliza, her reputation was as solid as the inn's.

As Martha J. Trist would remark many years later in 1901, "[Eliza] was a woman of much ability, & was known to, & respected by, Mr. Jefferson Mr. Monroe, & James Madison; these gentlemen all were her friends personally, and corresponded with her."[6] With Jefferson, it was a correspondence that lasted nearly half a century.

Frequent boarders of the House Inn clearly looked upon Mary House and Eliza with great fondness. Even when the men wrote to one another, their missives frequently included fondest regards for both women. In a letter to Madison from Joseph Jones on September 19, 1780, he asked for compliments to be passed along to the "worthy Mistress" and "the old lady" of the House Inn.[7]

This conviviality from Eliza and her mother, and a sense of home was surely welcome when Revolution rumbled and ricocheted within the State House, where Congress convened. As increasing burdens of taxes and grievances imposed by the King shook the Colonies, Mary House—embracing the importance of location, location, location—wisely moved her inn and tavern closer to the epicenter. Leasing a building at Fifth and Market Streets, just two blocks from the State House, the establishment became more than merely a place to eat and sleep. The House Inn's tavern and tables, like those of the famed City Tavern, were one of the pillars for end-of-day talks of politics over pork and Port.[8] How did such discussions affect Eliza?

Given the content in Eliza's letters penned throughout her life to a multitude of founders, it's clear that while she upheld propriety, there's rarely a hesitancy in sharing her opinions on politics, the country, and even personal or family matters. It's easy to extrapolate that one of two things was true of Eliza during those early Revolutionary days at the inn. Either she naturally engaged with the founders and boarders on such a wide range of subjects. Or she learned to.

During those years, a faithful Patriot was nurtured, and her position at the inn would both attract and influence another boarder. One who would become ever so much more dear. Nicholas Philip Trist.

A young Lieutenant from Britain in the (Royal Irish) Regiment of Foot, Nicholas was billeted at the House Inn as his regiment was posted in Philadelphia before the war.[9] Whether it was a love despite differences, or a young man in uniform having his head turned, the marriage between Nicholas and Eliza came in June of 1774 before the Army moved north.[10] By September, Nicholas was fatigued from endless marching with the regiment, and from Perth Amboy he writes to his "Dear Betsy," that "a letter from you My Dear will decrease my anxiety."[11]

By February 1775, a baby was due to arrive, and that prompted Eliza's first trip beyond her home town. A few months shy of her twenty-fourth birthday, she traveled to New York to give birth with Nicholas nearby. Upon the arrival of his own son, Hore Browse Trist, it seems that Royal uniform became ill-fitting to Nicholas, and he resigned his commission[12] in an effort to remain in the colonies and out of the impending war. He ventured eastward to homestead, eventually assuming land granted to him in Louisiana, in Natchez.

While his resignation and settling of that acreage is more his story, Eliza's tale continued in Philadelphia without him. She returned to the inn with their son, and as the Revolution took hold and it became increasingly ill-advised for a woman to travel over the Appalachians, at the inn she would stay. And so the years ticked by… 1776…1779… 1782…

By the time the Revolution ended with the Treaty of Paris in 1783, Eliza had spent more hours and days with Madison, Jefferson, and her mother than with Nicholas. Their son was nearing eight years old.

With boundaries more settled, travel over the mountains was more easily achieved. And yet, remarkably, Nicholas did not return to Eliza and his son to bring them south.

Instead, Eliza determines to uphold a request Nicholas espoused to her in his September fifteenth letter. "My Dear Betsy… You thought you had resolutions enough to undertake the Journey, if it has not or does not fail you and it is both easier and safer for you to come to me I would have you endeavour to put it in practice."[13]

As for how she was to travel or arrange it, in that same letter, he also leaves those details up to her, suggesting, "From your connections I should imagine you will not find it difficult to get a Passage to Fort Pit." [14]

One of those connections was particularly supportive of her undertaking such a voyage. In a December 11, 1783 letter to Eliza, Thomas Jefferson writes… "I think you will be a distinguished creditor if you pursue your wild Missisipi scheme."[15]

And yet, Eliza's belief in herself making such a journey is far more emotional. During the trip, she writes to Jefferson on April 13, 1784:

> "Whatever observations I am capable of making I shall not fail to communicate to you but when ever I see any think out of the common way if they are beautiful prospects my sensations are very singular I believe for I can hardly suppress the tears from starting from my eyes and I am lost in wonder."[16]

This *wonder* at what the western territories might offer a burgeoning country was a burning question among the forward-thinkers of Eliza's era. We see speculation about expansion by Thomas Jefferson, who, within days of his December 1783 letter to Eliza, also wrote to George Rogers Clark on the fourth. "Pittsburg and Philadelphia or Winchester will be the surest channel of conveyance… Some of us have been talking here in a feeble way of making the attempt to search that [Mississippi] country."[17]

As evidenced from her own letters, we know this included Eliza. She writes with apprehension in her December, 1783 letter, "It is a very great undertaking for me who never experiencd any hardships to ride over the Mountains this season of the year. I expect to suffer a little but this I am certain the fatigues of the Body can not be worse than that of the mind which I have experiencd in the extreem."[18]

She *knew* she was unaccustomed to travel. And she went anyway.

Deciding to leave her son with her mother, she spends months preparing, purchasing a horse, and arranging for a wagon to take her baggage.[19] As for her means for communicating her observations… Pen and ink, and a simple, brown paper-covered journal—nearly equal in dimensions to this book you now hold—which may have been purchased at her brother's shop.

And what delights her journal contain. Personal, environmental, and geographical details are included from the day she leaves Philadelphia on horseback in late December 1783 through arriving in Pittsburgh in January.

Mr. Fowler, a friend of Nicholas', who had also previously resigned his Royal commission,[20] is the guide she frequently mentions. As it was untoward for a woman to travel alone, a companion named Polly, whom she mentions only a few times, accompanies her the whole of the way.

At Pittsburgh, there is a break in her writings, marked only by an "X," (page 27) as Eliza impatiently waits for the winter to abate and the ice to break up to permit the next river-bound leg of her journey. Over the next few pages, she occasionally recounts a few experiences from her time in Pittsburgh. She picks up the pen again (page 32) as she boards a flour-delivery flat boat, leaving Pittsburgh in May of 1783. She faithfully makes daily entries throughout her voyage through the falls of the Ohio, and along the whole of the swift and often harrowing Mississippi River to Natchez.

Because Eliza edited the content as she wrote, qualifying her own statements and descriptions, we should classify this as a journal, not a diary. It was not a keepsake for her eyes only. It's a journal that she carried home to share, and which has now survived about a quarter of a millennium.

Now, you likely have two other questions burning in your mind. Why on earth haven't we *all* heard about Eliza and her journey, and why aren't we taught it as part of our early American and westward expansion history?

Aside from the obvious answer (the patriarchy), history took a toll on Eliza's letters and ephemera, making her history fray and thin like a scrap of antique linen. As her friends and family grew, married, moved, and died, they kept and destroyed letters, scattering her remaining manuscripts into a number of descendant archives. And over the years, as historians sought out information for biographies of the founders, Eliza's writings were read, lines pulled that mattered to those projects, and the letters once again shelved, too often without a thought to the author herself.

Only a few historians have examined her writings, and primarily as they pertained to research about travel narratives, journals, or letters. Jane Wells conducted extensive research on Eliza's letters and family. Annette Kolodny was the first person to publish the journal in 1990 as part of the book *Journeys In New Worlds: Early American Women's Narratives,* which included research on some of the letters between Jefferson and Eliza.

What you hold now is a brand new transcription, and the first book to house only Eliza's travel journal. This printing does not couple her writings with other travel journals or essays, or her other letters. Nor does it go into detail about the men around Eliza, or her life beyond her last journal entry on page 71, when she abruptly ends mid-sentence, on the first of July, 1784.

Why? Rather than inundate you, dear reader, with footnotes, lengthy scholarly observations, and a dissertation that takes you further from Trist herself, it's imperative you see Eliza House Trist's writings and words for what they were.

Hers.

I therefore believe it is my duty, within *this* volume, to do less. The only notations included in this new word-for-word transcription show where the journal pages were torn, or where her words—sometimes crossed through or smudged—were illegible.

Here, every entry is as she wrote it with her edits included as superscript. The pagination matches hers—although she only numbered the first five pages—and each line length matches her own. Each long, winding thought or expression has been typeset just as it was set down by her hand. Only the occasional illustrations and the map are new.

Eliza was not one to waste her pen and ink on a period, comma, or semi-colon very often. (And for me to insert them is akin to me inserting my own twenty-first century assumptions.) Consequently, sometimes a whole page has not one mark of punctuation.

For the first page or two, you'll likely stumble as you read it, somewhat at a loss as to where her thoughts and descriptions start and stop. At times it reads as though she is having a one-way conversation with you and has barely stopped to breathe.

Fellow historian, Lisa Francavilla, who is the Senior Managing Editor of the Papers of Thomas Jefferson: Retirement Series for the International Center for Jefferson Studies, gave me the soundest advice during one of our coffee discussions. She said, "The best way to really understand Trist's writings is to read her words out loud."

Like poetry. For they are.

Aloud, you can feel her cadence and meaning. Aloud, you hear her pacing and yearnings. Aloud, her detailed descriptions are more easily woven into her seamless narrative. For these reasons, like some poetry, the text is centered on the pages.

I encourage you to speak her lines as you read, or better yet, read her journal to someone else.

Rather than simply *hearing* what happened when Eliza went into the Mississippi territory more than two hundred years ago, you may come to better understand what this extraordinary eighteenth-century woman was daring to *say*.

By sharing her story with you, and you sharing it in turn, it's my hope we can firmly place Elizabeth House Trist among those already known in America's founding and expansion history, and add her voice and journal to our lexicon of what it meant to go west.

– Karen A. Chase

The Travel Journal

❧

I had no Idea that there [were]
such beings upon this earth.

E. Trist

[Pages 1 & 2 are lost to history]

dinner and at 6 o'clock PM arrived at [page torn]
put up at <u>Steels</u> tavern a very good [page torn]
Tea I went to visit my old friend Mrs James [page torn]
who received me with her usual kindness. she [page torn]
me to accept of a bed but as we intended to se[page torn]
early in the morning, I declined accepting h[page torn]
kind offer 24th arose very early with an inten[page torn]
to set of before Breakfast but it set in to snow [page torn]
fast which detained us till 10 Oclock; we rod[page folded]
before we baited our Horses the roads beyond [page torn]
description bad: we cou'd get no further that day [page torn]
than Elizabeth Town, which is 18 miles from
Lancaster: had very good entertainment at the
Sign of the Bear on the 25th left it before Break [page torn]
the weather moderated a little but very ruff ro^ads
[page torn]ross'd a beautifull creek about a mile before
[page torn] town call'd Swatana it tak[page torn]

4

[page torn] orse go out of a walk which makes our
[page torn] tedious – we arrived at Chambers
[page torn] on the Susquehanna at 3 OClock PM but
[page torn]d it impassable such quantity of Ice running
we wou'd attempt to put us over we were under
necessity of staying at the ferry House all night
people uncommonly obligeing but the House
[page torn]ry bad for the winter season not being finished
[page torn] were obliged to Sleep in the same room
[page torn]h Mr Fowler and another Man not
[page torn]ry accustomed to such inconveniences
slept but little, on the 26th Mr Chambers
got several more hands and with great caution
got us over the boat being full of Horses and
the rapidity of the current together with the
Ice made it very difficult to attain the other
shore my heart allmost sank within me for [page torn]
[page torn] are times I was appreh[page torn]

5

about a mile from the landing happen'd to [page torn]
down to the shore (He was the Gentlemen that [page torn]
me my Marching orders from Mr Trist)
Surprise was great at seeing me at such a
Season travilling. He insisted on our going
to his House, where we were kindly [page torn]
Hospitably entertained by himself an[page torn]
to whom he had been but lately marrie[page torn]
seems a very good Woman and has a [page torn]
fine Plantation. we had every ^thing good and com[page torn]
with a hearty Welcome. 27th after breakf[page torn]
we left Capt Simpson and cross'd a very pr[page torn]
creek call'd yellow Breeches; this part of t[page torn]
country affords many delightfull prospects
At ½ Past 4 OClock we arrive'd at Carlisle
put up at Mr Pollock's tavern a very gen[page torn]
House. He a very facatious old Gentleman [page torn]
[page torn]d his Wife a very good kind woman the [page torn]
[page torn] than I [page torn]

[page torn] a distance from navagation it was too
[page torn]d far to walk often we allighted therefore
[page torn] only judge what presented it self to me
[page torn] I pass'd I was surprised on entering the
town to see such fine buildings it seems they
[page torn] erected at the Publik expense for
[page torn]ks and Stores at present unoccupied
[page torn] 28th after Breakfast we set off we
[page torn] the pleasure of a ^fine clear cold day went
[page torn] 14 miles, put up at McCracken's tavern
Mr Fowler had business in the Neighbor
[page torn]d we staid the remainder of the day and
[page torn]ght the House tolerable. 29th after Break
[page torn]t we proceeded; the weather extremely cold
the morn'g but Soften'd towards the middle
[page torn] the day, we arrived at Quigleys before
[page torn]en the person who had Mr Fowlers goods
[page torn] possession: we were under the necessity of
staying all night, waiting to see the Pack-
horse men This place is situated on the
[page torn] y pretty [page torn]

the Mountains and discharges it self in to the
Susquehanna. This county, the last war
was the frontier. The old people of the House
entertain'd us with ^an account of their former suffering
being continually harrass'd by the Indians –
but they have lived to see an end to this ~~suffering~~
they are upwards of eighty and the old woman
told me she coul'd ride a 100 miles in one day
without being fatigued if she cou'd get a Son
that wou'd carry so far. they have but one Son
who is married and has a house full of children
they have given all up to this son and have a roo[page torn]
in the House he maintains them. it gave me
pleasure to see so much harmony subsist
among them: the sons wife told me they had
lived together fourteen years and she never
Saw the old people out of temper ~~illegible~~
they are very religious presbeterians: pray[page torn]
before every meal and after but their conver[page torn]
chearfull and happy[page torn] I believe if there are g[page torn]

people in the world they are to be found at

this place my heart over flow'd with benevolence

[page torn] it cou'd not be envy to see an old couple that

had live'd sixty years together endeavering to please

^{each other and} make every one as happy as themselves by their kind

^{attention} a true picture of rural felicity: God continue

to grant you his blessing my worthy old man

and Woman 30th the Pack Horse men did

not arrive: as the snow began to fall we concluded

[page torn]best not to wait least we shou'd lose the path

[page torn]ver the Mountain. after being kindly entertained

[page torn] proceeded on our journey, the Snow still

[page torn]lling very thick we were obliged to put on

for want of a ~~illegible~~ place to stop at that was

fit for a christian to put their head in at one

House we stoped to feed our horses, the family

was large a good farm and a mill, the buildings

[page torn]ood; ~~and~~ ^{but} every thing was so dirty that I woud

rather have slept out of doors. I don't believe

[page torn]any of the children had been washed

[page torn]they were born one of the girls was

allmost a woman: I had no Idea that there [page torn] such beings upon this earth. ~~I~~ we began to assend the blue Mountains at Clark's gapp it look'd a little tremendious as we had no guide, and the snow fell so fast that Mr Fowler was uneasy least he shou'd lose the paths but thank God we pass'd it with out any mishaps, tho we found it difficult to accomplish: the ascent more gradual than the decent, we arrived at Mr Elliotts in the Path Vally, in the evening having rode 25 miles a good day journey, all things considered, a good supper of Partrages and good Beds made some amends for the fatigue of the day.

– After having had a good nights rest on the 31st we set off the snow up ^to the Horses bellies. after riding 2 miles we began ~~illegible~~ to ascend the Tuscorora Mountain: found it as steep as the one we cross'd the day before but not quite so bad as some horses had broke the

road a little, upon the Summit of the Mountain
my saddle turn'd: it was with great difficulty I cou'd
stick up on the horse. Mr Fowler got down to
assist me, and was up to his middle in the
Snow. had I dismounted, I believe I must have
Perished: for I cou'd not have mounted again
and I am certain I cou'd not have walk'd 2 or
3 miles through the snow, it was so deep: on
one side of me was a thicket and on the other
the other a precipice; the cattle in the valley look'd
no larger than dogs. we sufferd another
inconvenience for want of a breast plate
to our saddles; for some places that we had
to ascend where allmost perpendicular
and our saddles slip'd so that we cou'd scarcely
keep our selves on by holding the main we
were six hours going 10 miles. to fort Lyttleton
[page torn] call'd from a fort having been erected there
[page torn]ast war for the Protection of the frontiers
[page torn]t at present there is nothing of it to be seen.
[page torn]it was much more agreeable we found

good entertainment. The house is kept by one Bind, who had been a Capt in the continental Service and knew how to live better than the generallity of back woods men. We left Fort Lyttleton on Newyears day rode 19 miles, came to the Juniatta in the morning found a difficulty in crossing. it being very deep and full of Ice. we were obliged to put up at the first House we came to which is not a license [page torn] tavern, but for want of such travillers are under the necessity of putting up there. The Man of the House is a Magistrate, and the laws of Pennsylvania prohibits such great men from retaling spirituous liquors therefore ^he only cou'd make out the bill, and his Wife receive the Money our entertainment the worst we had met with, not with standing the Man was a Colonel in the Militia. the whole House consisted of two rooms; the private room was occupied

by the Colonel his Lady and children the
other which serv'd as kitchen cellar and Hall
had two dirty beds: the one occupied by Polly
and my self was up in a dark corner surround^{ed}
by pickling tubs which did not yield the
most agreeable smell in the world the others by
Mr Fowler and a Lawyer Hamilton (who
came after us) on his way to the court at Harris
Town. a Nag driver his son and daughter
a Negro wench and two or three children
had the floor for their birth. for my part
I kept my cloathes on to keep my self from
the dirt off the bed cloathes: neither cou'd I sleep
for the crying of the children and the
novelty of my situation. we arose very
early and after paying our bill which came to
three dollars, for a supper of cold pork and
a bowl of Gin Gnogg and some sour buckweed
bread we left the banks of the Juniatta with
as little reluctance as any place we parted
from, tho the situation is very pretty

I was much pleased with the prospect of
the country which ^is Mountanious and, the river
Juniatta running ^through these Mountains for a 100
miles a clean beautifull Stream but only
navagable for rafts and that only in the
time of the freshes, it affords fine fish and
from its being shaded with evergreens its
beauty was much heighten'd at this season
I cou'd not but figure to my self that this must
be the Lethe tho the fields where not Elysium
We arrived at Bedford time enough for Breakfast
on the 2^d which is 15 miles from Colo Martins
This Village consists of about a 100 Houses some of
them very good it is built in a Vally, partly
Surrounded by a pretty Streem a Branch of
Juniatta call'd Rhea Stone the country
looks beautifull even in this dreary season
there is something enlivening and delightful

in the situation of this Town which seems in the center of a bason form'd by the surrounding Hills, we were so pleased with our entertainment that we did not set off till noon ^on the 3d for my part I cou'd with pleasure have staid longer we went no further than 13 miles stop'd at a little Hut kept by one Ryan the neatness of the place and the attention of the man made us as happy as if we had been in a palace – if we cou'd have been accommodated with a chamber to our selves but that was impossible the whole House was but one room built with logs no floor or windows a good fire served to give light to the house as well as to Warm it we had a little particion run along the side of our bed and we hung our great coats up at the foot which made our birth very private Mr Fowler and Mr Hamilton retired to the Kitchen for us to go to bed; and I made it a rule to get up before day light that I might [page torn] body nor they me dress, it is so customary for the Men and Women to sleep in the same room that some of the Woman look upon a Woman as affected that makes any objection to it. one told me that I talk'd to upon the subject that she thought a Woman must be very insecure in her self that was afraid to Sleep in the room with a Strange man for her part she saw nothing indelicate in the matter and no man wou'd take a liberty with a woman unless he saw a disposition in her to encourage him. Our entertainment was as good as if ^in a city; the man and his Wife had formerly kept a tavern in the city of Dublin, and are very assiduous and obligeing. The woman went on before us to a House she had about Twenty miles ^of to prepare for our accommodation the next day 4th after Breakfast we set out on our journey and soon began to ascend the Allegany Mountain it is call'd three Miles to the summit We found no difficulty, the assent being gradual we pass'd over some very poor barren land where there was plenty of game, but the land on the Mountain, in general, seems to appear very good. we stop'd at a farm house to feed our Horses the people were most all sick in the winter season the Woman inform'd ~~they was~~ ^that all ways some or other of the family were sick there is allways a mist which freeses as it falls and adds greatly to the beauty of the trees but I fancy the moisture of the air makes it unhealthy In the after noon we arrived at Stony ^Creek which is another beautiful Streem as wide as the Juniatta – Mrs Ryan prepared for our reception the House had been good but was allmost gone to decay having been deserted all the war as the Indians had murderd many families in the Neighbourhood we had a private room and in every respect much better accommadated than we had a right to expect so far in the woods upon a road that no person traviled during the war We left Stony creek on theMorn'g of the 5th

this days journey very tiresome there being
no house for us to bait our Horses at we found the
roads very indifferent we cross'd a fine creek call'd
Quimahone before we came to the Laurel Hill
and arrived at Fort Ligonier in the evening
after having rode 21 miles the weather mean
and a drisley rain through the whole day
and night 6th was waked in the Morning by
a pretty severe Thunder Storm and a very great
fall of rain which had melted all the Snow and obliged
us to proceed on our journey tho the rain still continued for fear the creeks rising shou'd detain us
for several days which we were given to understand
frequently happend in great freshes there being no
Bridges on the West side of the Mountains before
our departure I visited the fort it being esteem'd
the best Stockade in the Western Country there
is a bout out a Doz^n log huts erected within the fort
which the families in the Neighbourhood resorted
to when ever they apprehended danger from the
Sanagees, after Breakfast, we set off Ligonier is
Situated upon a creek call'd Loyalhanna there are

two or three dwellings besides those in the fort one of which General Sinclair formerly lived in at present un occupied we found very good entertainment at one Mr Galbreaths, the land in this Neighbourhood is very fertile and the country seems pleasant We found the Loyalhanna very rapid and allmost too high to pass with safety occasion'd by the melting of so great a quantity of snow Indeed ~~our~~ ^this days journey ~~was~~ ^has been as dangerous as any we had gone through the small runs as well as creeks were all most impassible. The Horses more frequently near swiming notwithstanding I did not feel much intimidated but plunged through with no other mishap than geting wet, the roads were very bad my horse cou'd scarcely keep his feet he fell with me once but I was so lucky as to keep my saddle Mr Fowler gave me credit for my good Horse manship. we were emersed in difficulties several times particularly geting through a Swamp about 9 miles from Ligonier Our houses were up to their Bellies and cou'd not move one foot which obliged us To dismount not being quite as heavy as our Cavilry and picking our way we got out without sinking higher than our knees in the mud, we arrived at Hannas Town in the evening after having rode 21 miles and a very disagreeable ride it was. The town consists of a Doz log huts it had been before the War much larger but a party of Brittish and Indians surprised the town, murdered several and carried of several families captives to Detroit some of the inhabitants saved themselves by taking refuge in a little Stockade and defended themselves with only fifteen muskets against 300 Indians and Brittish who signatured themselves by taking the Women and children and burning the town. The Courts are held at this place and unfortunately for us are siting at this time we found a difficulty in geting a place of shelter such a number of people being assembled illegible to attend the court Mr Orr the Sheriff was so kind as to give us a bed at his House which only consisted of one room and that on acct of his business as Publick as the Bar room of a tavern his Wife had a bed in one corner of the room we occupied the other, the poor Woman had been lately brought to bed and was very Ill she appeared to be a very delicate good Woman and had been comfortably situated

before the place was burnt I did not know what
to do about going to bed there being no curtains to
screen us from the sight of everyone that came, at
last we had recourse to our cloaks and blankets
which answered the purpose very well. the
Wind changed in the night to the NW, and in the
^morning of 7th the whole earth appeared like Glass and so cold
that we hardly had resolution to set out, but
necessity obliged ^us to proceed which we did after
Breakfast the roads were so Slippery that it made
it very dangerous riding we concluded to go
about two Mile out of the way to get our Horses
frosted the cold was so intense that I was allmost dead
we found it impossible to get to the next stage
which is 20 miles therefore hired a guide
to conduct us to a good farm house which was
but 10 mile where we were inform'd we couldn't be
provided with beds. we stay'd at a little cabbin
about half way to warm our selves and got a
good dinner it was evening before we
got to Waltowens the name of the owner of the
farm. We found a comfortable room warm with a
stove I felt quite happy for we were almost

frozed we had a good comfortable supper of fat bacon
fried and some Coffee I eat it with a mighty good
appetite we met Mr Irwin, a gentleman from Pitts
being at the House old Mr Waltonowens and Mr Irwin had one
of the beds Polly and I my self the other
but we found no difficulty in being private having
good worsted curtains round the bed we allways
made it a practice to dress and undress behind
the curtain therefore found no difficulty notwithstand
ing there were six or 7 men in the room Mr Fowler
and the rest of ^the people had some clean straw
spread on the floor I must confess I never
Slept better, in the Morng of the 8th after breakfast
we set of the weather still excessive cold our
Horses scarse able to keep their feet we stoped at
a little cabbin to warm our selves being almost
frosed riding only 5 mile. after getting a little thaw'd
we again proceeded on our journey our difficulties
Seem'd to encrease we were obliged to dismount at
every hill or run the risk of breaking our necks.
some times our Horses wou'd tumble and some times

[This page was left blank.]

our selves I had one tumble that hurt me a good deal: decending a very steep hill at the foot of which runs Turkey Creek, which is 12 miles from Pitts–g we found the creek so full of Ice as to make it at that place impossible for my part I wou'd rather have run the risk than assend the hill again notwithstanding the man who lived on the other side called to us not to attempt ^it unless we meant to lose our lives – we were obliged to go up the hill and ride a mile further up the Creek before we cou'd attempt to cross at last we got through but not without being in great danger, we got some dinner at at the Widow Myers and set of in hopes to get into Pittsburg before bed time we met with an inhabitant of that place at Waltowens Pollys Horse being in better Spirits than mine she push'd on in Company with this man. I cou'd not get my Horse out of a walk and every step his feet all most sliping from under him at last down we came, but lucky enough to receive no damage

only it made his cowardice increase and ~~made~~
aded nothing to my courage poor beast he
trembled every step he took after that night
came on and for the first time since I left home
my Spirits forsook me I began to prepare
my self for the other world and for I expected
every moment when my neck would be
broke I cou'd not help crying Mr Fowler
kept before me and it being dark I did not
expose my weakness some times I wish'd he
wou'd ride on and leave me so that I might get
down and <u>die</u> – at last we came to the Bullock
Pens a farm belonging to Mr Eliott I was almost
over come with cold and fatigue having been on
Horseback 3 hours and only rode 6 miles we
concluded to stay till Morning it was a bitter
night and a very bad house Mrs Elliott was
so kind as to part beds from her husband on
our account she wedged me in with her self
and child in a miserable dirty place she having

resigned her birth to M`r` Fowler I never lay so uncomfortable in my life the people were civil and did us a kindness by affording us a Shelter and put themselves to some inconveniences to accommodate us, or I cou'd say a great deal more in dispraise of our entertainment we got into Pittsburg time enough for dinner on the 9`th` of January. About 3 miles before you enter the town there are two roads the one to the right is call'd the Allegany from its vicinity to a River of that name the other is call'd the Monongahala lying to the left which likewise takes its name from a river We took the right hand road, and notwithstand`ing` the intense cold I was pleased with its beauty being situated on the banks of the river and that river had as Majestick an appearance as though it was near the Ocean it was quite unexpected to me to behold so large a bod of water at such a distance from the Sea

just as we enter the town Grants Hill
presents it self on our left hand it appears
to be about 100 feet in height – a sigh escaped
me as a tribute to the memory of those
poor fellows that was slain in battle at that place
[inset] A heap of dust alone remains of the
[inset] 'Tis what thou art, and rot that proud shall be.
Fort Pitt is situated up on a point of land
form'd ^by the junction of the two rivers with
the Ohio, for the Ohio appears to me to be
a continuation of the Monongahala
but the Alleghany meeting here with the
Monongahala take their course together and
form the source of the Ohio both rivers are
about a half a mile wide and the banks are
in most places about 60 feet high on the
Monongahala where the town is chiefly
Built there are about a Hundred buildings
all (except one, stone, and one or two frame)
are built of logs and they are in a very illegible

ruinous state. ˣ The Alleghany is a fine
clear and cold water the banks are not as
high as the other river neither is there
any declinity which makes the land fall
a way in the time of the freshes, there is a fine
orchard belonging to the Garrison a number
of the trees have fallen that were planted
near the water side about 12 feet was carried
away this Spring – but the other shore
receives it, which is call'd the Indian side
the land is exceeding rich and abounds
with an abundance of maple trees from
which they make quantitys of sugar
I pd a visit to their camps in the time
of their sugar harvest which is as soon
as the sap begins to rise, and was much
pleased with the excursion the vegetation
being much quicker on that side of the
river presented to our view a beautifull verder
a sight that we had been stranger to for some
time, the low land lying between the river and the

high lands on hills, is call'd bottoms and nothing
can exceed the quallity of those grounds in
the month of May they look like a garden such
a number of beautifull flowers and shrubs
there are several wild vegatables that I wou'd
give the preference to those that are cultivated
Wild Asparagus Indian hemp stepchild sprouts
lambs quarters &cc – besides great abundance
of ginsang, Gentian, and many other aromatick
on the other side of the Monongahala the
land is amaizing lofy tis supposed that
the whole body of it is cole and goes by
the name of cole Hill at one side it has
been open'd to supply the inhabitants with
fuel it is equal in quallity to the N'castle
or any other I ever saw The hill is seven
Hundred feet perpendicular and on the
top is a settlement the land is fertile and
capable of raising all kinds of grain
the timber is very large and the shrubbery
pretty much the same as is produced

in the bottoms. the prospect from this
Hill is very extensive and if the country
which is mountanous was cleared ~~illegible~~
it wou'd be beyond discription beautifull
Grants Hill is a delightful situation I think
I wou'd give the preference for to live on
as you are more in the World the view
is more confin'd but the objects are not
so deminitive below you – . The fort is situated
upon the point or near it formerly it was
a very elegant fortification but the English
when they abandon'd the post in 73 destroy'd
it and the present one is built out of the ruins
the Barracks one of Brick but poor pacth'd
up things the Gates ramparts &cc – seem
to be sufficiently strong to answer their
intended purpose as a protection against
the Indians – there are so many hills that
command it that if it was much stronger
I fancy it cou'd not make any great resistance

against a ^few good piece of Artillery in the spring of the year the rivers abound with many fine fish some of them exceeding good particularly the Pike which greatly exceed those that are caught below the mountains in flavor and size some of them weighing thirty pounds the cat fish are enormous some of them are obliged to be carried by 2 men the perch are commonly about the size of Sheep heads but they have been caught that weigh'd 20 pound there are several other kind such as herrings, &cc – but different from ours the bass look more like our sea perch only much longer and I give them the preference to all the rest for their delicacy of flavor. upon the whole I like the situation of Pittsburg mightily and was there good Society there I shou'd be contented to end my days in the Western country I made an excursion over the Monongahela to the Cherties settlement about ten miles from Pittsburg where Mr Fowler has a fine tract of land laid out in farms

The Cherties Creek is the most serpentine of any
I ever saw, in the course of ten miles we had to cross it
five or six times. here and there farm woud present it
self to our view with a few acres around it cleared but the
country is yet in a very rude state it wou'd
afford many beautifull prospects it being Hilly
and the land of a superior quallity – for my part
I felt oppress'd with so much wood towering above me
in every direction and such a continuance of it
a little opening now and then, but a very confined
Prospect nothing but the Heavens above and the
earth beneath and a pretty spring bubbling
every here and there out of the side of ^a hill.
I began at last to conceit my self Attlass
with the whole World upon my shoulders
My spirits were condenc'd to nothing my head began
to ach and I returnd to town quite sick —
May ye 20th left Pittsburg with as little regret as
I ever did any place that I had ~~illegible~~ lived so long in… Mr & Mrs
Fowler treated us with every possible attention, and from
the number of strangers resorting thither on their way

to the Cumberland &cc made the winter pass a way much more agreeable ^that it otherwise wou'd we where at several dances at which there wou'd be fifteen or twenty ladies and as many Gentlemen – if there had not been those little recreations I shou'd certainly have been very miserable. the tardiness of the boat builder detain'd us till the river got so low that I was in great trepedation least our passage wou'd be stop'd but good fortune has attended us. three days of rain have swell'd the rivers and we have the flattering appearance of a speedy voyage our accommodations all things consider'd not to be complain'd off the weather pleasant and every things wears a smiling aspect – we soon came to Mackees Island 4 miles from Pittsburg it appears to be about a mile in length and very fertile as is most of the land in this country. about three miles further is another fine Island nam'd Montiers seven miles long it is a Very fine tract of land. I am inform'd that <u>Montier</u> has sold it to several ~~different~~ people at different Times. This montier is the decendant of a f rench man

and Indian he has nothing but the external politess
of the former, his habits and disposition bespeak his
origin from the Mother being a savage in every
sense of the word. The Ohio is full of small islands
therefore must omit particularizing not being acquaint[ed]
with their names – if any they have, We arrived at dark
at fort M[c]Intosh having come 30 miles it was
noon when we left Pittsburg — there is a Sergeants
guard kept at this place but the night is too far
advanc'd for us to se what kind of a place it is
we had a comfortable dish of tea and at about
9 OClock in preparing for bed I unfortunately
fell from my birth backwards bruised my head
and shoulder and otherwise hurt ^[my self] sufficient to make
me a little more carefull in future however
I got a pretty good nights rest and in the morng
Of the 21st we were Eighty miles on our way
at noon we reach'd Wheeling which is a Hundred
miles from Pittsburg we went a shore for milk
there is the remains of a stockade and a few log
Houses one of them a very good one w occupied by

a Mr Zane who owns a good deal of land in this
Neighborhood which is very rich and the situation
high yet the people seem to have caught the infec–
–tion of the country, a desire for Kentucki
I am allmost in extasy at the Magnificente of ~~illegible~~
display of nature, the trees are deck'd in all their
gay attire and the earth in its richest verdure
So much for blooming May
22^d after a good nights rest we arose had
a comfortable breakfast by 9 Oclock got as far
as the Muskingum 171 miles from Pittsburgh a fine
River about 300 Y^{ds} wide and about 200 miles in length
takes its rise from a swamp about 40 miles this
side lake Erie, passd the little Kanhawa at noon
it appears to be about 150 y^{ds} wide along the
banks of the river just at that place is a
great quantity of very large stone supposed
to be of an excellent quallity for mills stones
equal to the french Burrs –
23^d 9Oclock in the Morng came to the

great Kanhawaa or new river a beautiful –
situation for a town the point is clear'd and
the banks are high there was a very pretty fort
at this place ~~and a~~ till about 4 years ago it was
destroy'd by the savages The land is the property
of General Washington – we came 100 miles in 21
hours and drifted all the way 1Oclock ᴾM pass o
the Guyandat, we have not yet seen any Indians
but it is thought dangerous to go ashore as they
have been seen lurking about this part of the
river we have not seen any wild beasts till to
day a bear presented him self to our view but he made
off before our people cou'd get a fire at him
at sun set we were as far as sandy creek – our
troubles I am ~~afraid~~ ᵃᶠᶠʳᵃⁱᵈ are going to commence a very
severe shower that has we our beding Polly taken
very unwell with a severe and I had headack which
alarms me lest it may continue. This evening has
all the appearance of rain.
24ᵗʰ a very fine morng after a very dreadfull
night Thunder and severe lightning and exceeding

heavy rain our birth made very disagreeable
the roof let in the water in several places –
we pass'd an Indian camp in the night we could
hear them yell but it was too dark for us to
see them. 8 oClock in the morng pass'd the Lioto
it appears to be a very pretty little river, one can
hardly be a judge of what width the rivers are
for they are so shaded with large trees that
the view is contracted — The Wind against us
and very high which obliges us to make fast
to the shore for the first time. I amused
my self gathering ginger which grows
in great abundance a long the banks, ~~we
had~~ the wind has abated a little, and we are
enabled to proceed on our voyage only havg
laid by one hour Pollys fever returnd towards eveng
however we had a tollerable good night
25th the morning clear but the wind against
us which impedes our going very much we
pass^d the little Miami after dark 126 miles from
the Lioto and licking creek at t 11 Oclock

26th a fine clear cold morning the wind in our favor at 7 Oclock pass'd the Big Miami it is a fine river the banks much higher and more clear'd than any of the rivers I have seen except the big Kanhawa there are numbers of creeks continually presenting themselves and some of them very large and what is extraordanary when ever you see a creek on one shore there is always another directly opposite noon came to limestone creek the big bones are found three miles from this place back in the Woods – the difficulty attending my getting there for want of a guide and other obstacles obliges me to give up all thoughts of satisfying my curiossity tho we shall stop to wait for some of our people who have been out to hunt for several hours the wind being so much in our favor our boat makes so much way that we are apprehensive they will not be able to come up with us after regaling

our selves with a walk on the shore for half
an hour our hunters return'd with out any game
which was a disappointment as we expected to
have had some fresh meat for dinner — there are
such numbers of boats continually going down
the river that all the game have left the shore

Pass'd the Kentucke 11 Oclock at night had
not the opportunity to see it but am told it is about
the size of the great Kanhawa there are no
Settlements upon the river – which surprised
me, such a number of people having gone to that
country I expected to have run the lands about
here well inhabited, but it seems they go up
~~this~~ ^the Kentucke river about 100 miles before they come to
the settlements

27th arrived at bear grass creek
six oclock in the evening about a half a mile
from ~~illegible~~ Louisville the great number
of boats that lay up the creek and several
families that were encamp'd at that place
~~illegible~~ made me think I had

got in to the world of spirits – We were met by
several Gentlemen that I had the pleasure of being
acquainted with – who conducted us to the fort
where Mr Taylors family reside for the present.
our accomodation not the most desireable – in
point of elegance being an old log hut Mrs Taylor
her four daughters polly and my self occupy this
place as a chamber we spread our beds at night
and in the morning by rolling them up they serve
as seats, an old barrell with a bord on the top
is our table and this is comfortable ~~and a
illegible~~ to what many are obliged to put up
with. the polite attention of the Gentlemen
to serve us renders our situation as agreeable
and more so then we have any reason to expect
The Fort has been a very good one but is now out
of repair there are 12 habitations within the
encloseur the Town is laid out in lots but not many
buildings erected what there is hardly deserving
the name of Houses – but so necessary is a shelter
that a little cabin about 12 feet square lets for
six and eight Dollars per month. The situation

of this place is very pretty. the bank high
and commands a view of the falls and Islands
at any other time I shou'd take much more
satisfaction in examining the beauties of
this place, but my mind is at present not
in a very tranquil state, our boat is fast on the
Rocks and it is doubted wether she will be
got off. this spot is reckon'd unhealthy
owing ^to the springs, which are impregnated
with copperness yet the inhabitants are so perverse
that they will use this water because it is cold in
preference to the river – I observ'd some ponds of
Stagnated ^water particularly the ditch round the
Garrison which must contribute to the unhealthiness
of the place – 28th our boat took a pilot to go over
the falls but either his villinay or carelessness run her
on the Rocks which occasion'd us great uneasiness
the owners and people great fatigue being obliged
to unload her and the current so amasing rapid
that they with great difficulty accomplished it in

the space of eight days the expense attending
this unfortunate event was upwards of fifty
Pounds – we were treated very kindly by Mr Taylors
family and indeed by everyone in the place – but my
mind was not at ease, the waters of the river was every
^day decreasing and I was under great anxiety lest we
should be detained till the Autumn. I did my
endeavor towards disappating those gloomy
thoughts by joining in several little dances that
were made on the M^iss Taylors and our accounts
I experienc'd the greatest attention and politeness
from several Gentlemen – and particular marks
of friendship from Colonel Anderson and
Colonel Lewis of Virginia and a Mr Trant
a young Gentleman lately from Ireland
and has lately open'd a store at this place
nine oclock in the morning 5th of June we left the falls all matters
righted in our boat the day too warm to be
agreeable and what Wind there is against us
the river appears to more advantage this side

the falls then above – the shore seems cleaner
and in many places for about a mile in
length there is a regular Wall to support
the bank as if built of the first hewn stone
one of our men went on shore to hunt and
being gone several hours returned with a deer
the first wild meat we have had – Sun sets
Pass'd salt river which runs up in the
Kentucke settlements as they are call'd
I am informed there are a number of good
Plantations up on this river – at 10 oClock
made fast to the shore for the night for
fear of geting aground as there are many
sand bars in the course of a few mile
the river is low which will lengthen our
voyage very much we go but 30 mile in a day
and above the Falls we went 50 —
6th after a very disagreeable night tormented
by Gnats and Musquitos we left our
moorings at the dawn of day, very severe

thunder gusts all the Morning. – in the after
noon we went on shore in the canoe at the
Point of an island to hunt for turtle eggs
this Island is of sandy soil and abounds
with grape vines — which they say are
very luscious when ripe we did not
succeed in getting eggs, but caught a fine Gosling
along the shore there is a great quantity of
stone that look like Iron ore I dont think
the land very remarkable from the falls to
this place which is about 70 miles the timber
not very large at least upon the water side
and I have no opportunity of seeing any other
heavy rain all night – we pass'd the Green
river about two oCclock in the Morning of
the 7th about nine it began to clear and
our people went on shore to hunt and kill'd
a tame cow which they mistook for a Buffaloe
however it turned out to be very good Beef – They

employed all the rest of the ^day jerkin it to
prserve it, which is done by cutting it into
small thin pieces and running them on sticks
lay them on a scaffold underneath they make
a small fire and a great smoke which in a
few hours drys so as to keep a long time
8th in the morng rain but cleard up
warm and continued so all the day nothing
remarkable but passing a great many Islands
and geting into very shoal water on a sand
bar, we were very apprehensive our boat woud
ground but with great care we got clear —
We pass'd a fine large river about Sun set
which I conclude to be the Buffaloe, none of
our people ever remmerberd to have seen it
before, having I suppose gone by it in the night
the owners of the Boat seem to be well acquainted
with the Rivers this being the fifth time they
have gone down the Ohio 'tis the largest river
between this and the Allegany – I was alarm'd
about noon seeing our boats crew geting their
Guns in order — for fear the Indians shou'd

attack us – several of them being encamp'd on the Shore and our boat was under the necessity of making fast directly oposite to them the Wind being high made the river so ruff that our boat cou'd not stem to waves – I must confess I was well pleased when we again put of which we did in about an hour – the weather a little moderated This part of the river is thought to be the most dangerous. the Indians keep along her more than any illegible where else but we have been very luck as yet, not having seen any to be certain off till to day

9th a bad night on account of the Musquitoes not to be borne, employ'd our selves in making a Pavilion out of some course gause I bought for that purpose at Pttsburg am in hopes this night will be something better than the last as we shall be able to keep of our teasing visitants for they have allmost done for me already

10th just before sun rise we pass'd the
Wabash a very fine river which runs
500 miles in to the country there are very
fine french settlements upon this river
one about 180 miles up call'd the OPost
I am inform'd the country is very healthy
and the land very fertile and that
it is a place of considerable trade about
8 oClock we observed two canoes with Indians
making towards us – we were prepared for
their reception if their intentions had been
hostile – the boat in company hail'd them
and invited them to come on board one of the
canoes accepted the invitation Two Indians
a very neat and handsome squaw with a young
child of they had formerly been of the Delaware
tribe but a number of them had left that
nation about fourteen years ago and went to
live up the Wabash They have been our
very great enemies this War, one of the

fellows calls him self James Dickison he
is one of their chiefs, and a sensible fierce
looking fellow, but his character is very
bad, they say he has plunderd several boats
and murderd many people that have been
going down this river, my curiossity led
me to visit them as they had all the appearance
of friendship – they eat and drank and smoked
the calumet – as it is good to have friends
at court I carried the Squaw some bread
and as her Infant was exposed to the sun
I gave her my Hankerchief to shade it, for
which she seeme'd very thankfull – M.^r McFarlan
gave them some flour and meat and a bottle
of Whisky, <u>to make glad come</u> after honor
ing us with their company for about an hour
they wish'd us well and left us in great good
humour – We arrived at the Big Cave early
in the evening and went on shore to see it

I lament that we had not a little more day
light that I might examine it more minutely
when the river is high it stands directly
on the waters edge but that happens not
to be the case which embellishes the
Prospect much, ~~in the~~ by presenting us
with a fine flight of steps of white stone
^that has the appearance of marble clean and elegant directly in front
of the Cave which appears to be about
forty feet high and sixty in width and
resembles an old castle – the entrance
is as large as a common door to a house a
grape vine runs up on each side and
a tree juts over the top which adds
to its beauty. it was so dark that we were
obliged to set fire to some light wood to
see our way in to the cave – the open
part of the passage is about four feet wide but near
^the earth the rocks jut out so as to make the path only
a foot and a half – I was disappointed not finding

more room, as the passage indicated something
capacious, but ^the widest part does not exceed seven
foot the driping of the water form'd some –
petrifactions that resembled columns – we soon
hurried out for the dampness made it diˢagreeable
up on the whole I think it one of the most
grand and beautifull natural structures and
the greatest curiossity I ever beheld – there
is a fine smooth perpendicular rock for a
bout a quarter of a mile nearly joining the Cave
which looks as if it was built for a garden
Wall it appears to be about 20 feet high – after
we got into the canoe to go on board the flat
by one of the people extending his voice ^we observd that
there was an amazing, echo, we diverted our
selves for some time; every word that was
spoken was repeated as distinctly as if a
little girl on shore was mocking us – for my
part I cou'd hardly be persuaded but what

some people had encamped on the shore
after we got to the boat – the wind began to blow
which obliged us to make fast to the shore
for the night, ~~the~~ which was so fine and
lucky that we were not troubled as
heretofore with Musquitos
11th the wind lull'd but the weather very
warm about 10 oClock was alarm'd by a canoe
making for our own boat which we supposed
to be Indians, the blunderbuss was mounted
the Muskets loaded, and every matter properly
arrainged for fighting – my self disposed of
between the flour barrells – but to my great
satisfaction they turn'd out to be some french
men going to the Cumberland river to trade
their appearance was perfectly savage
having little or no cloaths on and their
hides quite as dark as the Indians – they
had come from the OPost – at 9 OClock in
the evening we reach'd as far as the
Shawanoe on Cubmerland river, it is

a large river and runs a great way into
the country I am inform'd that it takes
its rise from the Allegany Mountain in
Washington county Virginia the
meandering of the river makes it above
two thousand mile to its source we pass'd
the Chinokee River in the night
12th a fine Breeze but the wind as usual
contrary which makes our passage tedious
in the morning, we came to the Massac a
place where formerly there had been a fort
and was evacuated by the french in the year
58 the land is remarkable good about here and
very fine hunting grounds – our people went
on shore to hunt, but coming to an Indian
camp where there were some squaws they did
not think it prudent to fire though they saw
a drove of Buffaloe and two deer – about
noon a heavy cloud that portended
a storm made our Gentlemen think it prud^ent

put to shore and very lucky for us we
did – for in all probability our boat woud have
Store on greatly damaged for a more violent
wind I never heard – the trees crack'd about us and it
thunder'd and lightned and rain'd as if heaven
and earth were coming to gether for an hour
after which, all was again calm, and we proceed
on our voyage but very slow the current
very dead supposed to be the back waters
of the Mississippi – made fast to the shore for
the night as it is thought unsafe to enter
the Mississippi in the cark
13th after a pleasant cool night very few
Musquitoes to trouble us I arose in expecta^tion
of seeing the Grand River but had not
that satisfaction till four Oclock in the
afternoon, the day pleasant and the wind
in our favor – up on any other occation I
Shou'd be sorry for the exchange – the

Water of the Mississippi uncommonly low
so as to discover a large sand bar near the
junction of the two rivers, but the current is
much stronger then the Ohio – about 3 miles
below the mouth of the Ohio, there is a fort
or, rather the remains of one which was erected
by the Americans this War. and call'd after
Governor Jefferson I was inform'd it at present
was occupied by a Nation of Indians call'd
the Ta^uras who have been nutaral notwithstanding
the English took great pains to make them take
up the hatchet against us – to avoid their
Snares they abandon'd their grounds on the
Miami about 60 mile from Detroit and came
down to this part of the country – Mr Berind
and two of the men went on shore in hopes to
get a hunter, I was eager to accompany them
I wish'd to see the fort be cause it bore the name
of my friend, but I was dissuaided from making
the attempt as it was not certain what Indians

might be there – they returned unsuccessfull
and gave me a very unfavorable account of
the place which they found totally abandon'd
and the worst situation of any up on the
river the land very low – we anchor'd
about 7 miles below the Ohio the evening
cool but no comfort till we got under our
<u>bear</u> for the Musquitos, the navagation
of this river is renderd dangerous by a
number of logs that are fix'd by one end
at the bottom of the river and the other
end is about two feet about the water many
boats are lost by running upon these logs
and the greatest attention is necessary to
avoid them, however we are happy in
being with carefull good men well acquainted
with the river

14th at dawn of day we left the shore and
soon came in sight of the Iron bank a great
quantity of ore may be picked up on the surface

of the earth. it is 16 miles from the Ohio
a fine high situation – and I am told there
is to be a town laid out here very soon at
ten oClock we pass'd Reed creek 12 mile
from the Iron banks – we saw some elk
on a sand bar our men went on shore and
pursue'd them in to the thicket and kill'd
two of them but it detain'd them so long
that they had to row 30 miles before
they reach'd the flat – in the afternoon we
got among the Canadian Islands there are
nine of them, and one so call'd from a number
of people on their way from Canada down this
river having stop'd there for some time the
last Island we came to we observed the
channel on both sides to be bad on account
of the fallen timber which rear their heads
above water and some of them being less
steady than others the force of the current
makes them bow which as fix'd upon

them the name of sawyers we got in
the midst of them, and I have not words to
express the horrors of our situation
for my part I resign'd my self up, expecting
our boat wou'd be tore to pieces but with
great exertion we got through them
we stood in great need of the two hands that went
on shore to hunt our boat being but weakly mor'd
I dont like this river the passage is attended
with much more danger than I had any Idea
of – we are obliged to make fast every night
and the banks are so high the current so rapid
and the river close to the shore so fill'd ^with fallen
timber and brush that it is attended with ~~with~~
great difficulty to accomplish. they were
several hours before they cou'd make fast
for the night and at last were obliged to
tye the boat to some floating wood in eddy
water. as it happen'd to be a calm night we
lay very well till morning

15th shifted our quarters to a more secure haven the place we are at is call'd Loncela Greece the best hunting ground any where on the river – as our provisions are allmost exausted tis agreed to lay by the day in hopes of kill.g some deer – the men returnd with out even having fired a gun – I lament the loss of this day as the wind has ^wou'd have been in our favor the river is rising which affords us some satisfaction – every one thinks their troubles the greatest, but I have seen so many poor creatures since I left home whos situation has been so wretched, that I shall begin to consider my self as a favord child of fortune, here is a poor family encamp'd at this place. a man and his Wife their father and Mother and five children, left the Natchez ^four months a go on their way to cumberland river and had not a morsel of bread for the last three months they had buried one the oldest of their sons a little while before – the poor little children when they saw us cry'd for some bread, our Gent. gave them some flour – and I had the pleasure to contribute to the happiness of the Women by giving them some tea and sugar – which was more acceptable to them than diamonds or pearls – 16th left Lance La greece which is 80 miles from the Ohio the river has risen 3 feet which makes us go briskly – we pass'd two Glades the only clear land I have seen except where some person had been living we made fast at Sun set after having gone 80 miles – 17th after going 20 miles we were obliged to make fast to the shore the wind contrary and very high it happen'd to be a clear good bank which enabled us to go on shore had the pleasure to see the wind favor some tho not kind to us for a large boat with all her sails set with a Doz^n men at the oars come up the river quite fast they left N Orleans

3 months ago bound to the Illinois – one Oclock
P.M. the wind died a way and we push'd our luck
again – the Musquitos bite and tease me so
much that my life is allmost a burther to me
I do sincerly think that all the wealth of
the Indias wou'd not induce me to live in
a Musquitoe country – I had no Idea they cou'd
possibly be so intolerable – we did not go
more than 15 miles before we were obliged
to make fast to the shore for the night
18th the wind still against us, we came
to the first of the Chickasaw Bluffs about
Seven oclock in the morng which is 201 miles
from the Ohio – my patience is allmost exausted
what with the Musquitos and head winds
I am allmost sick the passage early in
the Spring woud be pleasant but at precent
there is nothing but trouble – I have various
Ideas about this river – some times conceit I am
got to the lay end of the world or rather that
it is the last of Gods creation and the Seventh

day came before it was quite finnish'd; at other
times I fancy there has been some great revolution
in nature and this great body of water has forced
a passage were it was not intended and tore up
all before it – the banks are now about 50 feet
high very ragged and every here and there great
pieces ^of the earth tumbling in to the water after great trees go
with it, which fill the river with logs some place's
^long shore there will be great rafts of fallen timber
the water is as muddy as a pond that has
been frequently visited by the Hogs. alltogether
its appearance is awfull and Melancholy
and some times terrific – one oClock P.M.
came to more of the Bluffs 12 mile from the
first we pass'd – they ^are high red banks and
look as if the earth was impregnated with
copper ore – the Chickasaw Indians are settled
back of this place they in company with

with some refugees robed several boats at
this place, we came in sight of the last of
the Bluffs at sun down which is 45 mile from
the first and made fast for the night
19th the wind so high and against us
that we cou'd not attempt going till noon
when the wind greatly moderated we found
a difficulty in passing the Bluff apoint of
an Island made the channel very narrow
and look'd as if two waters met which caus'd
a whirlpool our boat went round like a top
and alarm'd me a good deel a little while
before having been inform'd that last year
a Mr Lankasang lost a boat at this very
spot with 600 barrells flour on board He dash'd
against some raft wood that happend to be
lodged there at that time and sunk directly
but fortunately for us the coast was pretty

clear. we went about 30 miles, when we were
obliged to lay by an hour sooner then we wood
have done some heavy clouds appearing that
indicated a storm – but its progress was
not so rapid as was expected. this is a
Passionate sort of a climate ~~soon~~ ᵠᵘⁱᶜᵏˡʸ raised
~~and~~ ᵇᵘᵗ soon blows over – however this was
not so easily appeasd, it began about 10 oClock
and seem'd to vent its utmost fury the whole
night in all my days I never saw such a
continuence of sever lightning and heavy
rain, a most uncomfortable night – I am
so stung with the Musquitos that I look as if
I was in the hight of the small pox I have
taken every precaution to guard against
them to very little purpose and I am in
a continual fever with the effects of their venom
20th no rain but cloudy and warm at noon
found ourselves a little mistaken in our reckoning

we came to the last Bluff and we thought we pass it the day before our progress very slow a week this day since we enterd the Mississippi and have not got 300 mile –
21st we went very well till noon when we were obliged to lay by for a for a couple of hours for a storm of wind and rain after it abated we again set of sun set as usual made fast to a fine high sand bar the most agreeable mooring we have had no bushes to harbour the Mosquitos we were not troubled quite so much
22^d Pass'd the river of St Francis 6 oClock in the morng which is 75 mile below the lower Bluff about 10 came to a very pretty glade full of fine ripe plumbs there are great quality of them growing in this country but I dont think they are as large as those that grow in Pensylvania in

the Evening Mr Gibson and M^r McFarlane
with three of the hands set of for Noahs
ark a spanish fort about 12 leagues
up the white river as they had heard
that ^the people of that Garrison were in want of flour
23^d about sun set we arrived at white
river and made fast to an Island to wait the
return of our canoe this day very pleasant
and fewer Mosquitos –
24th a very long day waiting the
return of our people this Island is full of
young willow trees, which smell very –
fragrant a large boat ~~in sight~~ from the
Illinois – encam'd on this Island for the
night – they are going down the river to
take off some people who lost their boat
three month ago
25 about 10 oClock in the morng
our people return'd having sold 100 barrells

at 17 Dollars p^r barrell they got unloaded
by noon and we again proceeded on our voyage
there are a great many Pelican ^about here the first we
have seen they are a fine Majestick looking
bird and at a distance resemble the swan
one of our people kill'd one and brought it
on board the boat they are all white except
the wings which are tinged with black
it measured ten feet from the tip end
of one wing to the other the Bill is about
a half an inch wide and a foot in length
the under jaw on bottom of the bill resembles
white leather and expands in an extraordanary manner I saw 14 quarts of water
put into its mouth and it wou'd have held more
I can not comprehend what use they make of
this amaizing pouch unless to scoop up
the little fish they are very harmless and
so tame that they swim allmost in reach
of our oars. the most curious bird I ever

saw – we pass'd the Akanza about 5 Ocklock
in the evening went about seven mile
before we lay by for the night which
made our days journey 25 mile an estremely
warm day and night allmost coddled
26th the weather the same
I can hardly keep my self a live the
river has risen three feet which is a
cordial to my spirits as it facilitates
our going –
27th so eager are every one to
proceed that we left our moorings so
early that we went 7 or 8 mile round
an Island when we might have saved
so much by waiting till day light
the weather exceeding warm about
5 oclock in the afternoon came to the great
Cut point. the water by frequently over
flowing the land here has made a channel
illegible line of text

there appears to be several of them with
in a few years has made a passage through
a point of land of a few hundred y^{ds} which
cuts of 30 mile – here we saw the poor french
men who had their boat sunk – we gave them
the good news of their boat being near at hand
28th the wind in our favor very
reviving to me for I am every day more
anxious to be at the end of my journey or
voyage in the afternoon our boat by
the violence of the current was drove
against a large tree that was about
20 y^{ds} from the shore it held us by
the roof notwithstanding the water run
so rapid as to carry every thing before
it if the boat had not been very strong
we shou'd certainly been cast a way they
were obliged to cut a way part of the roof
before we cou'd get disengaged for my
part I gave my self up I did not even

see a probability of saving my life
for the other boat was some miles
a head of us and I thought the canoe
was crush'd to pieces but that was not
the case We weatherd the encounter
we met some french going noahs ark
29th at 8 oClock in the morning
we came to the Yasow a long river
that makes at the back of an Island
the passage is difficult at this place
there is another cut of and the
water is allways very ruff in that
case and requires great exertions
to keep in the right channel this cut
of is 90 miles from the great cut point
which is 108 mile from the Akanza
we stoped at an Island for the night
and I lost my poor little dog Fawnis

tis supposed the Alligator got him
as one was seen swimming about the boat
in the evening – poor little fellow
30th at 10 oClock came to the great
Gulph which is 75 mile from the Yasow
This is the first settlement we saw on
the river tis the property of Capt Borber
at present occupied by a Mullato Woman
Nam'd Nelly she was exceeding kind to
us gave us water mellons green corn
apples in short every thing that she had
was at our service her conversasiton
favord rather more the Masculine
than was agreeable yet I cou'd not
help likeing the creature she was
so hospitable she gave us the history
of her life she may be entitled to merit
from some of her actions. but chastity is
not among the number of her virtues

after spending a couple of hours with Mrs Nelly
we took our departure and in the afternoon came
to the little gulph – 18 miles below the G Gulph
there was a fine Plantation at this place
belonging to Phil Allston but at present
it is quite abandon'd he being concern'd in the
revolt at the Natchez was obliged to fly
the country – The imprudent conduct of a
few designing men has allmost broke up the Natchez
Settlement and ruind many that were elegantly
settled – we went 15 mile before night
I was attackd with a violent headack and so
Ill that I got up in the night and took a dose of
tarter which in a few hours greatly relieved
me it was lucky for me that I did for in all probability
I shou'd have had a violent fever –
1st of July a fine cool pleasant ~~day~~ Morning
within a few miles of the Natchez – my heart
sinks within ^me and I feel so weak that I can hardly
keep my self a live • what can cause these sensations

my journey is most compleated three days more
I shall be happy – in sight of the Natchez
will write to Mr Trist perhaps a boat
may be just seting of and he will be glad
to meet me I know – as our boat is to be
detain'd to unload some flour…

> my journey is most completed three days more
> I shall be happy — in sight of the Natchez
> will write to Mr Trist perhaps a boat
> may be just setting off and he will be glad
> to meet me I know — as our boat is to be
> detain'd — to unload some flour

The last entry from the journal.

Beyond the Journal

The journey of Eliza House Trist was far from over after her last entry on July 1, 1784. And her long life was far richer than this journal attests.

I am cataloguing her manuscripts and packaging her life story in a more widely accessible narrative work for the general public, investing time and resources in research, travel, databases, archival copies, and publishing.

If you'd like to know more about Eliza's life post-Natchez, or you want to help her story become more widely known, here are two ways to help:

- If you believe you or your family, or your local archives, might have manuscripts or information relating to Elizabeth House Trist,* please contact me. It takes a village of boots on the ground to walk into the past. *Visit: KarenAChase.com/contact*

- Please purchase authorized copies of this journal to share with friends, family, teachers, and students. Every dollar of proceeds is going toward the Eliza Project. *Visit: KarenAChase.com/books*

*Eliza signed her letters E. Trist, but she may be referenced through other versions of her name including: Mrs. Trist, Elizabeth House, Eliza House, Elizabeth House Trist, Eliza House Trist, Aunt Trist, Betsy Trist, etc. Naturally, she may also be archived with ancestors, her husband, or descendants.

Endnotes

1. Christ Church (Philadelphia, Pa.), "Baptisms, marriages, and burials, Christ Church, 1750-1762," Philadelphia Congregations Early Records, accessed April 19, 2024, https://philadelphiacongregations.org/records/item/ChristChurch.RectorsRegisters_BaptismsMarriagesBurials1750-1762_v030

2. Samuel House Will. Case No. 42. Pennsylvania, City of Philadelphia, administration files; Philadelphia(Pennsylvania). Register of Wills; Probate Place: Philadelphia, Pennsylvania

3. Ibid.

4. "Memorandum Books, 1783," Founders Online, National Archives, https://founders.archives.gov/documents/Jefferson/02-01-02-0017. [Original source: The Papers of Thomas Jefferson, Second Series, Jefferson's Memorandum Books, vol. 1, ed. James A Bear, Jr. and Lucia C. Stanton. Princeton: Princeton University Press, 1997, pp. 525–541.] Other boarders at this time were James Madison, Daniel Carroll, Ralph Izard, and William Floyd of New York and his family (Papers, vi, 226 description begins Julian P. Boyd and others, eds., The Papers of Thomas Jefferson, Princeton, N.J., 1950- description ends ; Madison, Papers, vi, 182).

5. The Pennsylvania Gazette, 7 July 1784.

6. Martha J. Trist Burke's Notes on Trist Family History, [ca. 1888–1901] | Jefferson Quotes & Family Letters, Monticello.org. Martha J. Trist Burke Commonplace Book, privately owned.

7. "To James Madison from Joseph Jones, 19 September 1780," Founders Online, National Archives, https://founders.archives.gov/documents/Madison/01-02-02-0059. [Original source: The Papers of James Madison, vol. 2, 20 March 1780–23 February 1781, ed. William T. Hutchinson and William M. E. Rachal. Chicago: The University of Chicago Press, 1962, pp. 91–92.]

8. Historic Resource Study Independence Mall: The 18th Century Development Block

One Chestnut to Market, Fifth to Sixth Streets; Anna Coxe Toogood, Historian Cultural Resource Management, Independence National Historical Park, August 2001; pp. 43-44, and 56.

9. Commissions of Nicholas Trist as ensign and as lieutenant in the 18th (or Royal Irish) Regiment of Foot. Albert & swirly small reference. Box 3

10. Deposition of Alexander Fowler to the Birth, Baptism, etc of Hore Browse Trist (born Fe. 22, 1775) Son of Nicholas & Elizabeth, Philadelphia Sept 26, 1787. University of Virginia, Charlottesville, Albert & Shirley Small Special Collections, Papers of the Trist, Randolph, and Burke Families 1721-1969, Box 2

11. "From Nicholas Trist to Mrs. Trist, September 15, 1774," Albert & Shirley Small, Trist Papers, Box 1

12. Deposition, Albert & Shirley Small, Trist Papers, Box 2

13. "From Nicholas Trist to Mrs. Trist, September 15, 1780, " University of Virginia, Charlottesville, Albert & Shirley Small Special Collections, Papers of the Trist, Randolph, and Burke Families 1721-1969

14. Ibid.

15. "From Thomas Jefferson to Eliza House Trist, [11 December 1783?]," Founders Online, National Archives, https://founders.archives.gov/documents/Jefferson/01-06-02-0307. [Original source: The Papers of Thomas Jefferson, vol. 6, 21 May 1781–1 March 1784, ed. Julian P. Boyd. Princeton: Princeton University Press, 1952, pp. 382–383.]

16. "To Thomas Jefferson from Eliza House Trist, 13 April [1784]," Founders Online, National Archives, https://founders.archives.gov/documents/Jefferson/01-07-02-0092. [Original source: The Papers of Thomas Jefferson, vol. 7, 2 March 1784–25 February 1785, ed. Julian P. Boyd. Princeton: Princeton University Press, 1953, pp. 96–98.]

17. "From Thomas Jefferson to George Rogers Clark, 4 December 1783," Founders Online, National Archives, https://founders.archives.gov/documents/Jefferson/01-06-02-0289. [Original source: The Papers of Thomas Jefferson, vol. 6, 21 May 1781–1 March 1784, ed. Julian P. Boyd. Princeton: Princeton University Press, 1952, p. 371.]

18. "To Thomas Jefferson from Eliza House Trist, [ca. 8 December? 1783]," Founders Online, National Archives, https://founders.archives.gov/documents/Jefferson/01-06-02-0300. [Original source: The Papers of Thomas Jefferson, vol. 6, 21 May 1781–1 March 1784, ed. Julian P. Boyd. Princeton: Princeton University Press, 1952, pp. 375–377.]

19. Ibid.

20. Deposition, Albert & Shirley Small, Trist Papers, Box 2

The Fonts

The fonts used to design the print version of this journal were specifically chosen to add to the reader's experience.

Geographic Script

Used in the chapter headers and on the cover, the font was created by Gilles Le Corre, an engraver from France. His lettering is based on historical research, relating to engraving styles from the 1700s.

ADOBE GARAMOND

Originally developed in the 1600s in France by Claude Garamond, this font would have been used in a multitude of books—some of which Eliza Trist may have read. It's used for main paragraphs and the journal. Versatile, and graceful, it's also eco friendly. The letterforms use less ink than other similar faces.

HELLO PARIS

Designed by Latsayz and Angga Suwista, vintage font creators, it's used for Eliza's full name on the cover. The timeless, swooping letters are an homage to the Mississippi River.

Acknowledgements

I am incredibly grateful to the Virginia Foundation for the Humanities for the 2019-2020 fellowship that gave me the time and space at the Library of Virginia to commence my project, beginning with the Eliza House Trist journal. With the insights and support of historians like John Deal, Lisa Francavilla, and John Ragosta, this project began and continues in earnest.

For Richard Trist, and the descendants who've reached out to me as a result of that fellowship, your willingness to share stories and your desire for more have been the fuel to release this journal so we can hopefully have more eyes focused on the hunt.

To my sisters in the Daughters of the American Revolution, I'm grateful for all you do in inviting me to speak about Eliza, and in championing the stories of this extraordinary woman and her mother.

Mary House is now officially recognized as an NSDAR Patriot, which has officially made her daughter, Eliza Trist, a DAR. (That project is a whole other story. Let me just offer a million thanks to everyone who made the application and paperwork happen, especially Ellen, our newest member.)

My thanks to Katie Drash Mapes for her ad-hoc research and the remarkable spreadsheet I never wanted to build. You've given me time and an organized way to access documents to build this publication.

And always to Ted, my travel companion and compass.

– Karen

Also by the Author

Fiction
Carrying Independence
Mary Angela's Kitchen

Non-Fiction
Bonjour 40: A Paris Travel Log
Brand the Author (Not the Book)

About the Author

Author. Speaker. Independent Historian.

Karen A. Chase's historical novel, *Carrying Independence,* was awarded number 12 of *Shelf Unbound*'s Top 100 Indie Books of 2019, and was a nominee for the 2020 Library of Virginia Awards.

She was a 2019-20 Academic Fellow through Virginia Humanities at the Library of Virginia, which began her research into the journey of Eliza House Trist. The author is a member of the National Society of the Daughters of the American Revolution and James River Writers.

She has spoken with historical and corporate audiences in the US and Canada. She travels for research and joy, and writes from Richmond, Virginia.

For books and speaking requests:

KarenAChase.com

www.ingramcontent.com/pod-product-compliance
Lightning Source LLC
Chambersburg PA
CBHW022042160426
43209CB00002B/34